Richard,

> "Thanks to your book I can now display great service in my restaurant!"

> ---Francis Le Roux , Owner, De Ark Guesthouse, Lydenburg, South Africa

Richard,

> "This publication has a lot of great organizational tips helping us to elevate our dining room customer service!"

> ---Orlando Campos, General Manager, Brasilia Grill, Montville, New Jersey

Richard,

> "Your book was very helpful for the dining room organization at our new restaurant!"

> ---David Ray, Food and Beverage Director, Radisson Hotel, Annapolis, Maryland

How To Improve Dining Room Service

Includes a Restaurant Performance Evaluation Guide

Richard Saporito

www.topserveconsulting.com

Toll free: 888-276-4808

authorHOUSE®

AuthorHouse™
1663 Liberty Drive, Suite 200
Bloomington, IN 47403
www.authorhouse.com
Phone: 1-800-839-8640

First published by AuthorHouse 7/3/2008

ISBN: 978-1-4259-8274-4 (sc)

Library of Congress Control Number: 2006911108

Printed in the United States of America
Bloomington, Indiana

This book is printed on acid-free paper.

Table of Contents

This handbook is an easy learning guide that will have immediate positive effects on your restaurant dining room customer service. Since there are very few references to consult for some fast basic knowledge on the intricacies and nuances of restaurant service, I have decided to explain it on paper in a very concise manner. The guide will help you create the basic steps toward quality and efficiency, which is essential for pleasing diners and gaining their repeat business.

Before installing any new system, a needs analysis of dining operations must be conducted because every restaurant is unique in its own way. Strategies that work in one restaurant may not work in another. For example, some restaurants may choose not to take any reservations at all because they are always extremely busy; therefore, a no-reservations policy works best for those establishments.

There are many different service levels and styles that are particular to each restaurant, so I've kept these tips as general as possible. Please make sure all implementations are done with attention to detail.

If there is disagreement or an explanation needed about any concept, please feel free to e-mail me at topserveconsulting@msn.com, and I will do my best to provide a satisfactory answer.

Definition: "Moment of Truth" – An opportunity whereby a customer forms either a good impression or a bad impression about the service quality in a particular business or company. Millions upon millions of "moments of truth" occur out there in the customer service world, but the successful businesses register the highest percentage rate of good impressions. It means everything to their image and reputation.

Let us say that everyday you have the choice to buy the daily newspaper at two different stores within walking distance of each other. If only one storeowner always smiles and says thank you, then most likely, you will keep returning there to buy the newspaper—simply because of this short positive time period.

"Moments of truth" must be managed indirectly by creating a customer-friendly work environment where the main focus is to satisfy all of the customers all of the time, without anyone leaving dissatisfied.

This guide is designed to improve the percentage rate of positive "moments of truth" that take place in your business.

Note
For easier reading:
Host   =   Maître d'
Staff   =   Dining Room Customer Service Staff
             (Managers, Waitstaff, Bussers, Food Runners, Hosts)

Tip #1:   The Front Door and Reservation Desk

Improving the Front Door and Reservation Desk procedures, including Reservation Taking, Seating, and Host Responsibilities.

- At a minimum, the Reservation Desk must have space for the telephones, menus, Reservation Journal and Daily Sheet, floor diagrams, employee telephone list/schedules, restaurant business cards, a daily message book for important notes/telephone calls, toothpicks/candies/mints, etc. The Reservation Desk should include drawers to store items such as extra pens, scratch/dupe pads for order/note taking, extra menus (also paper menus to help market the restaurant), telephone books, and incident/accident report forms, etc.

- The Reservation Desk should be kept neat and orderly at all times as it can become quite disorganized during the busy hours.

- The host must dress nicely, be neat and clean, and always be upbeat, friendly, and helpful to customers. An experienced host once said that the purpose of guest seating is to make "Every table seem like the best table in the restaurant!"

- There can be simple opening and closing sidework procedures for the host, such as wiping down the menus or cleaning the front window.

- The telephone should be courteously answered stating the restaurant's name and asking, "May I help you?" Whenever taking a dining reservation, one must politely ask for the name and the number of people in the party, date and time of the reservation, and the contact telephone number. Also, special requests should be noted, such as birthday guests, high chairs, customer food allergies, or the need to be seated at a specific table or location in the restaurant (for example, far from the window on a cold night; close to the window on a beautiful day). This information must then be recorded in a

Reservation Journal that eventually will be transferred onto the Daily Reservation Sheet.

- On the Daily Reservation Sheet for each work shift, there must be plenty of blank lines for both the Customer Reservation Information (as stated above) and the Dining Room Table Waiting List Customer Information.

- The Waiting List must include the name and number of people in the party, the exact amount of wait time for an open table stated to the party, and the exact time the party was told the wait time. During the busy hours, this helps to organize customer seating overflow, which patrons appreciate while waiting to dine.

- Any cancellations must be immediately crossed out in the Reservation Journal and on the Reservation Sheet. These must be kept neat and well maintained, as quality dining room customer service depends on this information.

- Before each work shift, an <u>Employee Position List</u> must be made of waitstaff, bussers, food runners and hosts with their names and respective work positions. The list must include the numbered wait-station assignments (#1, 2, 3…) and restaurant dining areas.

- The Employee Position List information must be written on the Daily Reservation Sheet at the Front Desk, and posted in strategic locations for <u>all</u> staff to easily view. If this is done diligently, it will elevate the dining room awareness and communication level, especially in larger restaurants.

- To begin the timing process for guest seating, specific dining room tables should be allotted to incoming parties by placing reservation cards with the names and reservation times on the tables. It is a good idea to keep the waitstaff informed of their future large party reservations throughout the shift, so they can prepare to handle their customer flow properly.

- As the host, it helps to visualize the incoming customer traffic and seating process before and during the shift, seeking to reduce customer overload in all dining areas. Steady, even seating ("staggering") should be maintained with each waitperson receiving approximately the same number of diners.

- Traffic flow times vary from restaurant to restaurant, especially when factoring in the restaurant concept plus the food and service quality levels. If the restaurant and/or host are new, it may take a little time to learn how to gauge the times for dining room table turnover. Large parties usually stay longer than small parties.

- If a waitperson is overloaded with too many tables at once, incoming diners should be steered (using gentle persuasion) to the slower waitstations for better service. Overloading waitstaff with too many tables at once should be avoided. However, in some cases, it is not be possible, because customers must always be allowed to sit wherever they choose, unless specific tables have been reserved for other guests.

- If time allows, the host can record the number of guests seated per waitstation to help gauge the evenness of customer traffic flow, thereby balancing the seating process. It may not always be an exact system, but it does exert some degree of order and fairness at the Front Door. However, in very large restaurants, it could be too overwhelming at the Front Door to accomplish this system.

- During busy hours, customers waiting in the lobby or sitting at the bar can be offered menus to pass the time. In some restaurants, hors d'oeuvres are served to customers who have been waiting a long time for an open table. All ways and means must be exhausted to prevent customers from leaving to dine at another establishment—even if it means offering some complimentary items.

- If the host/management is not busy seating customers, they can purvey the dining room for customers in need of service and relay such information to the waitstaff. This is up to the discretion of the host, for they should never stray too far from the Front Door.

- Depending on the restaurant, if the host/management is too busy to answer the telephone, then waitstaff who are not busy should be requested to help in answering. Often, the calls are simple location/direction questions, or the taking of a reservation.

Definition: "No-show" – This means a dining party (large or small) calls the restaurant to reserve a table for a specific time, which gets recorded in the Reservation Journal. But then, the party does not show up for their scheduled reservation without even calling to cancel.

> *Parties of ten or more should be called by the restaurant to confirm their reservation.*

This will greatly reduce the amount of no-shows, which can hurt sales, especially during the busy hours. To set up a large party, two, three or more dining room tables may have to be utilized. If this large party does not arrive or call to cancel, revenue and customers may be lost during the holding period.

It is at the discretion of the host/manager as to how much extra time a table will be held for a late-arriving party that has not called to state their delay time. It is a judgment call, depending on the dining room floor volume and the number of patrons on the waiting list at the time.

Restaurant Situation: – Let us say the host is holding up three tables for a party of 12 and announces that there is a 20-minute waiting list for the next open table. Upon hearing this, some waiting customers choose to leave. If that reserved party of 12 never shows up, revenue will be lost, as the diners who chose to leave could have easily been seated at those three party tables.

It only takes one phone call to confirm a reservation, yet this lack of communication can cost hundreds of dollars or more in one night. Think of the yearly loss if it happens regularly! I see restaurants make this simple procedural mistake all the time.

Often times, small restaurants cannot afford the revenue loss from a large party no-show; therefore they should consider asking for a deposit.

For each situation discretion should be used, with the goal of never losing potential customers.

<u>Outdoor Seating</u>: – Outdoor seating can be tricky because unpredictable weather plays a role; therefore, outdoor seating should always be on a "first-come, first-serve" basis.

Weather permitting, outdoor dining is always highest in demand with outdoor seats usually filling up before indoor seats. In this case, you should completely avoid reserving any tables for customers regardless of the party size. On a beautiful night, newly arriving customers who are eager to dine outside will not enjoy waiting for a table, especially if they have any view of those empty outside reserved tables. They just may walk out to find another restaurant.

If used, a "first-come, first-serve" policy should be strictly enforced because customers, without knowing, will often call in and ask for a reservation outdoors. They should politely be informed of the policy, and that they increase their chances of getting an open outdoor table by arriving at the restaurant as early as possible.

***At the Front Door, one is dealing with individuals where all different types of situations can unexpectedly arise. Common sense, quick thinking, and good manners will help improve the restaurant's dining room service, reputation, and sales.

Every dining establishment is unique in its own way. It takes time and experience in coming up with creative ways to maximize table usage. The main goals are to minimize costly mistakes, maximize revenue, while at the same time delivering and maintaining a proper level of customer service throughout the dining room.

Tip #2:   Product Knowledge

Increasing waitstaff product (food/beverage) knowledge, ultimately leads to better service and higher sales.

<u>Definition: Menu Desciption</u> – a listing of each dish describing the ingredients, method of preparation (grilled, roasted, pan-seared, etc.), and accompanying side dishes/garnishes. A menu description can also be done for wine (by the glass and bottle) and beverages (special martinis: cosmopolitans, apple martinis, etc.)

The menu descriptions (with the kitchen's assistance) and wine/beverage list descriptions must be printed up and handed out to all waitstaff and food runners. There must be extra copies available for future waitstaff and food runner hires.

If the above instructions are followed properly, the waitstaff will know all about the menu, which is their greatest selling tool. If a customer inquires about a food or beverage item, the waitperson must be able to answer quickly and efficiently (saving time during busy hours) without having to interrupt another busy colleague who may or may not know the answer. With excellent menu knowledge, waitstaff can alert customers with regard to dietary restrictions and food allergies as well.

There should be a simple description for the wine list so that food and wine pairing tips can be mentioned by the waitstaff. A menu description for beverages will help upselling of special brands of vodka, gin, tequila, brandy, etc. Menu knowledge plays a huge role in upselling that translates into higher sales for the restaurant and higher tips for the waitstaff. If the waitperson is asked a question about a bottle of wine and cannot respond properly, then the customer may skip ordering that wine, not wanting to chance it. The customer may order only a glass of wine—or nothing at all—simply because some confidence has been lost in the restaurant and/or the waitperson. Using common sense and proper timing, waitstaff should always be suggesting cocktails, appetizers, and desserts in a subtle and unobtrusive manner.

***By precisely informing patrons about menu items, waitstaff will make positive impressions ("moments of truth") on customers who will then order with confidence. Improving menu knowledge is such a simple thing to do, which is why it often gets overlooked—with customer service and sales suffering as a result.

Tip #3:   Dining Room Awareness

Improving staff awareness, communication, and customer service procedures.

Tip #3 gives the dining room service staff "a sense of where they are," which is extremely important especially <u>if the restaurant is new or if the staff is new to the restaurant</u>. Tip #3 enhances the ability to communicate in "restaurant language," which, in turn, improves service procedures all around.

<u>**Definition: Customer Position Points**</u> – Basically, any customer in the dining room can be identified by a particular table number and a particular seat number. This can be done in any given dining room with the exception of perhaps a few tables, because of an awkward seating arrangement. These tables will not be a problem as long as all staff knows the arrangement and position points ahead of time from the floor diagrams.

It is most important to establish customer position point #1 for each table. The easiest way of determining the position point #1 is to have the customer's back directly in line (or as close as possible) with a particular location in the restaurant, such as the kitchen, bathroom, or perhaps a particularly visible item of décor. Every diner whose back is closest to this particular location or decor can represent position #1. Try to keep the location simple and easily distinguishable for all dining staff. After position #1 is established, move clockwise around the table, identifying each customer as position #2, 3, and so on. If a seat is empty, assign it a position anyway, as a guest may be arriving late. The main objective is that the person serving the food/beverage does so accurately and easily—which is much more likely if there is prior knowledge of the tables and seat numbers ahead of time.

If customer position points are not used, waitstaff, holding hot and heavy plates will be calling out dishes to customers because they don't know the position placements, wasting precious time and energy. Moreover, the diners, often in mid conversation or laughter, will be unnecessarily interrupted. This is one of many problems that will arise without using position points.

Dining Room Floor Diagrams, with correct numbering of each table and position point, must be very clearly printed and handed out to all dining room service staff, with extra printed copies available for all future staff hires. These diagrams must be placed in strategic locations for all staff to easily view, but preferably out of the customers' sight. The first table in each column or row should begin with "1" such as 11, 21, 31, 41, etc. for easier counting.

The Reservation Desk must have all of this information available for the hosts/managers on the Daily Reservation Sheet.

The staff can communicate all customer needs in the dining room by using the table numbers and seat positions. For example, if a customer at table #45 position #4 requests coffee from the host, the information can be relayed quickly and concisely to the waitperson working that table.

If the **Employee Position List** is drawn up and understood by all staff, there won't be any precious time wasted during rush hours with unnecessary questions, such as the proverbial, "Who's on station #3?" This kind of question should rarely be asked, especially during the busy hours.

If all the proper work - shift information is strategically posted, then employees/management will have a better sense of awareness in the dining room and service communication will flow more effectively. Again, it's so simple—which is why it often gets overlooked.

***The reduction of wasted time, motion, and energy is an essential part of improving dining room service. Simultaneously, it preserves much needed stamina for the staff, as the eyes and brain work much faster than the feet and back.

Tip #4: Scheduling

Maintaining the schedule and keeping the staff tight and content, is essential for pleasing paying guests.

Staff scheduling is crucial and closely tied to customer service. In every way, a balance must be achieved by matching the dining room service labor needs to forecasted business.

There should be a system whereby the staff shift availability days can be communicated in writing to the person who makes up the schedule. A simple staff shift availability sign-up sheet, posted conspicuously, will do. Each staff member should work a balanced amount of shifts throughout the week. If the schedule maker is burning out staff members with extra shifts *or* scheduling too many staff members to work only one or two shifts, it will subtract from customer service. Usually, a restaurant will get more efficiency from staff members working three, four, or more shifts per week, rather than only one or two. However, at times one may have to bend this guideline to keep the work schedule filled, but it should be kept to a minimum. Constant communication with the staff while staying abreast of their available work shifts will facilitate the scheduling process immensely.

The person who makes up the schedule must be highly aware of the projected business in the restaurant. The schedule should contain the correct amount of labor needed to provide a proper level of service for each work shift. Seasonal aspects, (such as busy holidays/slow summers), special occasions, private parties, etc., must be figured into the schedule. Any outside activity that may affect business in the restaurant (such as food festivals, parades, etc.) needs to be taken into account. If there are separate dining rooms, the busy times must be properly forecasted for each room -- especially if one dining room is more popular than another, say, because of entertainment on certain nights or by showing off a special type of décor. If there is outdoor seating, the weather must be watched because it can change quickly.

Forecasting the incoming business helps to schedule the correct amount of staff, with the perfect balance always being sought. If there is light scheduling on a day that gets very busy, the dining room customer service will be slow and inefficient – affecting sales and reputation. On the contrary, if there is heavy scheduling on light business days, it will become frustrating for waitstaff who will be working very few tables while draining the payroll.

Generally, the schedule should start on a Sunday; therefore, it needs to be posted by Thursday or Friday of the previous week. Excel spreadsheet formats are great for scheduling organization. The schedule should be posted in an easily viewable location with enough copies available for all staff. Staff phone lists should be printed, copied, and made readily available to all. This improves communication, especially for work shift substitutions.

This leads to the substitution process for staff work shifts. There needs to be a Substitution Book readily available with blank spaces for names, upcoming dates and work shifts for the next 1–2 months. If a substitution is made, the information must be recorded with the date and shift time (a.m./p.m., etc.). The substitution must be initialed by both parties involved, and subsequently initialed by a manager, ensuring there are no mistakes in communication. Any mishaps may result in a shift not being covered.

Scheduling may look great for payroll cost control, but it must be remembered that dining room service staff are real people with real lives whose cheerful and efficient service is what restaurants depend on. The schedule maker needs to be understanding toward the staff's scheduling requests, but should not roll over and play dead (again, balance). It is impossible to please everyone 100% of the time, but a proper scheduling balance will truly have a positive effect on restaurant dining room customer service and staff.

***It is better for a service consultant or manager to handle the schedule at the initial phases of a new operation. In some cases, mature restaurants may let a senior member of the service staff handle the schedule because it is a better way to communicate scheduling concerns. Please use whichever system works best for the establishment, because the staff schedule is a strong part of customer service and should not be taken lightly.

Tip #5: Sidework

*Ensuring that the staff is well prepared with all of the
necessary tools needed for dining room operations.*

Sidework is the opening preparation of dining room customer service and the closing (cleaning and storing) of dining service areas and items. Each establishment will have slightly different sidework because of uniqueness, yet it always needs to be done properly in every restaurant.

- Sidework duties should be posted for all staff to easily view, station by station, with respect to day and night shifts. Sidework should be regularly checked by the manager before and after each shift, because it is another waitstaff tool that is needed to ensure proper service. Depending on the restaurant, for every work shift, items must be stocked such as coffee, tea, milk, cleaned and filled condiments, oil and vinegar cruets, filled sugar bowls, and salt/pepper shakers for the tables etc—all readily available for dining room service.

- The waitstaff must check their dining room waitstations ahead of time for properly cleaned table settings, linens, table tents, soiled/wobbly tables and chairs, including bases.

- Before each shift, table settings should be polished with some club soda or a little bit of hot water on the edge of a clean napkin. Outdoor dining areas should use roll-ups (silverware placed in tightly rolled up napkins) which guard against outdoor bacteria.

- For polishing, dining ware may be safely placed above safely contained hot water, letting the steam settle on the ware and immediately wiping with a clean napkin.

- The workstations should include office supplies such as stapler/staples, dupe/scratch pads, tape and properly functioning computers/credit card machines.

- Since the restaurant day has long hours, there should be specific and reasonable opening and closing sidework duties. A balance must be attained with special regard to business hours of operation and assigned labor, with each staff member performing approximately equal amounts of sidework duties at the appropriate times.

Example: If a waitperson is responsible for watching the Front Door to seat early arriving customers between 4 p.m. and 5 p.m. (before the host arrives for the evening shift), then sidework duties should not include running errands from the basement. This waitperson needs to be readily available at the Front Door to seat these early arriving customers.

Example: Closing sidework duties should not include the closing and cleaning of a restaurant area too early in the evening, especially if there's a chance this particular section may need to be used again by patrons and/or staff. It makes sense to leave this section as one of the last sidework duties to be finished by a closing staff member after dining service has completely ended for the evening.

***Sidework provides the dining room with preparation, safety and sanitary aspects making it a necessity for service quality and efficiency.

Tip #6:   Cross-Training

Increasing the versatility of staff members while emphasizing "teamwork."

Definition: Cross-Training – Interchanging work positions. Some bartenders can be cross-trained as waitstaff and vice versa. Hosts and food runners can be cross-trained with waitstaff as well.

- Cross-training keeps the restaurant job interesting, increases labor productivity, and gives employees more confidence as they take on added work responsibilities.

- Cross-training forms a well-rounded staff because it helps employees empathize with each other's work position and situation. Staff will work more closely in tandem when they understand each other's work needs and tendencies.

- Cross-training does not necessarily have to be forced onto the staff. In most cases, there will be sufficient response from staff members wishing to improve their versatility in the restaurant. It isn't necessary to interchange everybody's work position, though cross-training 10–15 percent of the staff works rather well.

- Instead of always hiring completely new waitstaff, employees can be promoted from within the restaurant operation itself. Experienced and hardworking food runners, bussers and hosts can be promoted to waitstaff after becoming proficient at their positions. In-house employees are much easier to train because of their familiarity with restaurant procedures and staff.

***Cross-training may give surprise help on occasion. For example, if a bartender is absent because of an emergency situation, there could be an immediate replacement on hand by a waitperson already cross-trained to work the bar.

Additional Tips:

Maintaining the quality and appeal of the restaurant dining room.

The "Huddle-up": – Before each shift, it is a great idea for the manager on duty to have a small meeting ("huddle-up") with the staff before the dining room becomes filled with guests. It is an ideal time for questions, troubleshooting and discussion about the restaurant in general. Also, it is a time for positive reinforcement and to inform the staff of any changes in dining operations procedure. Basically, the huddle-up helps to unify everyone before service commences, getting everyone working together.

Always listen to feedback from staff and guests as they have answers to many restaurant problems.

- A positive atmosphere can be created within the dining room using personality and common sense. If the staff is encouraged or rewarded for doing an excellent job, such as high check averages, consistently exceptional service, etc., they will transmit this positive reinforcement energy to their customers (who need and deserve it the most).

- It is important for the host/management to be involved with diners and staff, especially during busy times. Customer needs in the dining room should be communicated and coordinated to the staff in "restaurant language" through the table numbers and position points.

- Depending on the service system, if time permits, the host/management can get involved with some service tasks. For example, if the host/management is not very busy, it helps to take a cocktail order or to serve dinner plates to a table in an overloaded waitstation. Similarly, if waitstaff is not busy, they can take on some host/management tasks such as answering the telephone or seating newly arriving customers. Also, during the work shift, waitstaff that <u>are not</u> very busy should always be encouraged to help other waitstaff that <u>are</u> very busy. The basic idea is that all job tasks in the dining room overlap and everyone helps out when they can.

As they serve the public, waitstaff need to know that management is watching their backs and will help out if they become overloaded with tables. A lack of this instilled confidence will have a negative effect on staff morale, thereby reducing guest service.

***It is important to create a <u>positive domino effect</u> that will permeate throughout the dining room so that everyone is working together and helping one another. The best time to get it started is at the beginning of dining service when the staff needs it the most.

<u>Atmosphere:</u> – air temperature, lighting, and music.

- Dining room air temperature must be appropriate and checked throughout the night. As the dining room fills up with customers, the room temperature will increase a few degrees. A slightly filled dining room makes for lower temperatures. In both cases, thermostats should be adjusted accordingly.

- Lighting must be appropriate for the restaurant theme and the time of day. As nightfall begins, the lights must be lowered adjusting to the fading light especially if and when candles are lit. The lighting must always be adjusted very slowly with the customer barely noticing.

- Music volume level and choice must be appropriate for the restaurant theme and the time of day without offending guest conversation. As the evening progresses, music volume can be slowly raised since a higher volume is better tolerated later in the night. Do not violate any noise codes of the neighborhood.

Tip #7:   Traffic Flow Guidelines

Improving the restaurant traffic flow during busy hours.

- When in restaurant motion, stay to the right as much as possible when passing others, especially if objects are being carried. Staff must respect each other's workspace.

- Whoever is carrying an item(s) or tray gets the easiest right of way. Whoever is carrying the greater or more fragile mass gets the easiest right of way (most certainly if they are hot items, such as steaming pastas or hot coffee).

- All staff should use the following phrases often: "Excuse me," "Passing thru," "Behind you," "Watch your back," "Hot stuff," etc. The staff should communicate their location to each other whenever necessary because of the limited work space.

- In high volume restaurants with very large staff, "bottlenecking" can occur. This happens when a waitstaff line builds up to perform a particular service task, such as receiving cocktails from the bar, or using a computer or credit card terminal, etc. If this happens, it should be suggested to the waitstaff to change gears and perform other service tasks. Afterwards, they can return to the bottleneck area—hopefully to find that the line has subsided. However, sometimes a particular service task may be too highly time-pressed to be switched for another and must be performed immediately.

Tip #8: Sanitation

Prevention is the key here, as these tips work in conjunction with one another.

These tips are extremely important to ensure repeat business and must be included in service training.

At all times staff should seek to improve safety and sanitation, because it reflects the restaurant's care of paying guests.

Customers will not enter an eating establishment that has poor sanitary conditions in sight. Some floor dust or even a few breadcrumbs near the Front Door may prevent potential diners from walking into a restaurant. Sanitary conditions have an almost subconscious effect on the customer. Whatever the customer sees on the outside of the restaurant can affect how they presume the food is being prepared inside the kitchen.

So let's begin with staff personal hygiene. Then we can move on to ways of preventing accidents and injuries to guests/employees while at the same time increasing efficiency and organization of dining room service.

- All staff must be clean at all times (especially hands and fingernails), and be well groomed with long hair pulled back and tied. Beards, moustaches must be kept neat and trim. Uniforms must be clean and pressed.

- Fingers must never touch any part of the face or scalp during service. All staff must wash their hands with soap and hot water frequently throughout the work shift, especially after coughing, sneezing, eating, or smoking. If handling food, protective gloves must be worn. Any cut or open wound must immediately be covered with a clean bandage.

- There must be no smoking or gum chewing in the dining room. Staff must not wear jewelry or any objects that can easily fall off or get caught on something.

- Before exiting the bathroom, <u>all staff must wash their hands</u>. How the bathrooms are maintained is an overall gauge for restaurant cleanliness and makes a statement about the establishment. The bathrooms must be checked periodically throughout the night for cleanliness.

- All staff should clean as they go. If there is a spillage, anyone can wipe it up—not necessarily the person who did the spilling.

- All dining ware (dishes, glasses, utensils) and napkins must be spotless before serving to diners. They must be stored in clean containers, protected from pests, dust, or other contaminants. Before serving, receptacles of condiments should be wiped down with a warm damp cloth.

- Fingers must <u>never</u> touch any part of the dining ware where food or beverage can be transferred to a diner's mouth. All dining ware must be carried at the base, handle, or stem. Do not put fingers inside glasses or near their rims.

- Dishes must be handled with the thumb on the edge and four fingers on the bottom. Cups and silverware must be carried by the handles only. Glasses must be handled at the base or stem.

- A clean napkin must be used for carrying any clean dining ware, especially when very hot. When bringing an extra dish for a cold item, such as a salad, make sure the extra dish is not warm or hot. If necessary, rinse with cool water and dry with a clean napkin.

- Use a scoop or plastic pitcher to retrieve ice, keeping the handles out of the ice. Do not use a glass to scoop ice.

- The outside and Front Door area of the restaurant must have a clean appearance. Remove any debris. All tables, tableware, chairs, windows, doors and menus must be clean. Remove any damaged ones. This makes the restaurant more attractive to potential diners and should always be included in the beginning sidework.

Tip #9: Safety

Reinforcing these tips to your staff improves the safety of your guests and staff.

- All management and staff should be requested to anticipate any potential safety and/or sanitation hazards. If they are unable to take measures to reduce or eliminate them, someone must be notified who can.

- It is recommended to buy quality work shoes with as much traction as possible on the soles (rubber is best).

- Keep aisles and exits clear and clutter free. Push empty chairs away from aisles and into place at tables. Politely ask customers to move handbags, briefcases, umbrellas, etc. that may be blocking aisles or exits.

- Turn corners slowly and at an angle distanced from the corner. Proper placement of mirrors can reduce accidents around corners, especially on stairways where food and beverages are transported.

- Open doors slowly, and look before opening them—especially swinging doors. Do not stand in aisles, doorways, or block traffic flow unnecessarily. Do not abruptly back up or make sudden movements, especially in bottleneck areas.

- Pick up objects off the floor and wipe up spillage immediately. Strategically placed floor mats are very helpful in reducing the number of accidents—especially during inclement weather. Any spillage on a customer's garment should be noted in a brief report, and the cleaning bill paid by the restaurant. If the stain is small, try some club soda with a clean napkin.

- When placing any item on a table, make sure it is away from the edge of the table so it won't fall off. If candles are used, make sure they are clear of all objects.

- When carrying very hot items, inform people around you ("hot stuff" etc.), moving slowly and carefully. When serving very hot items, inform the customer ahead of time before placement. When pouring hot beverages, the cup must stay on the tray or the table—never with the customer holding the cup while you are pouring.

- Do not touch broken dishes or glasses. Use a napkin to pick up large pieces of glass and a broom with receptacle to clean up the rest. Do not use a chipped or cracked piece of dining ware. Do not serve food or beverage that was ever contained in such an item. Even a very small crack in a dining ware or glass is a place for bacteria to grow.

- When clearing or carrying, stack items evenly balanced on the trays, placing heavier items in the center and lighter items on the outer sides away from the very outer edges. Do not over-stack items; carry only what can be safely handled.

- If possible, use two or more containers/bus pans for soiled dining ware; use the top container for glasses <u>only</u> and the bottom container(s) for plates and silverware <u>only</u>. This will reduce the amount of breakage when glasses and plates/silverware collide.

- When lifting heavy objects, make sure you have proper footing and a strong grip, lifting with the legs while bending at the knees. Continue to breathe while lifting, but do not twist the back. Ask for help with very heavy objects, as a two-person operation always works better. Do not lift anything over a customer's head.

- Lifting equipment, such as hand trucks and dollies should be used whenever possible for extremely heavy items (great for stacking racks of glasses or moving bins of ice). Do not leave dollies unattended, and make sure they are safely stored when not in use.

- There should be a well-stocked first-aid kit with plenty of Band-Aids, antibacterial spray, and burn spray available. Heimlich maneuver posters for aiding a choking person must be strategically placed and easily visible.

- CPR kits should be made available.

- Fire extinguishers should be in good condition and well placed. Exit signs should be well lit.

***Management must investigate all unsafe conditions reported by staff and take corrective action. This includes any conditions that may affect public safety, food/beverage safety, building safety, etc.

Emergency Procedures

Whenever there is a serious accident or extraordinary situation that affects the customers or staff, the restaurant personnel must use as much care as possible in dealing with individuals during these situations. This helps to eliminate any negligence on the restaurant's part, which can create enormous problems later.

- If there is serious danger at hand, do not panic. Call the authorities for help. Emergency phone numbers should be readily available.

- There should be standard written procedures for emergencies particular to each establishment and location. Incident report forms should be readily available to fill out with spaces for exact dates, times, names, and explanations (location, conditions, and corrective action taken).

- Do not begin an interviewing process until the situation has calmed down and after medical treatment has been dispensed.

- Take statements and write down the facts, revising them later for conciseness. If necessary, take photographs of the scene. While interviewing other witnesses (diners, bystanders, staff), be non-confrontational and objective without speculating as to fault or cause.

- Fill out a claim report and send it to the insurance company immediately.

***Incidents must be documented quickly and objectively. Keeping all records on file will help eliminate future problems, as management is responsible for the investigation. Primary focus should be on the specific cause, and on helping to prevent similar incidents from ever happening again.

Dining room service staff functionality and training is a continual, highly repetitive process, yet extremely important for a restaurant's survival. This operational manual will aid in that continual training process because restaurant management and staff always need efficient service systems to work within.

Use this publication wisely as an enrichment tool for your restaurant.

Richard Saporito, President
Topserve Restaurant Consulting Inc.

www.topserveconsulting.com

Toll free: 888-276-4808

Ten For Service
Ten "To Do's" Before Each & Every Shift

1 - Transfer all shift Reservation information from the Reservation Journal onto the Daily Reservation Sheet.

2 - Check the Substitution Book for any staff shift substitutions, then fill out and post the Employee Position List.

3 - Check the staff Sidework duties.

4 - Check the Front Door/Reservation Desk and dining room appearance with respect for cleanliness and safety.

5 - Allot specific tables in the dining room for the Reserved Parties with respect to specific Reserved times.

6 - Check the tables, chairs, and dining wares for cleanliness and placement.

7 - Check to see if the "86" lists are updated from the kitchen and bar.

8 - Check the bathrooms for ventilation, cleanliness and stock.

9 - Check the staff for cleanliness - uniforms, hair, etc.

10 - Hold the staff "Huddle up" to discuss restaurant related issues, policy changes, "86" updates, and to instill positive reinforcement onto the staff.

Topserve Restaurant Consulting
50 Question Multiple Choice Exam
<u>Test Your Knowledge of Dining Room Service!</u>

Choose the best answers for the dining room service questions:
(The correct answers with explanations are at the end of this exam.)

1) Define "Moment of Truth:"

a) Moment whereby a customer can form an impression about the service quality in a particular business or company

b) Moment before the customer arrives at the restaurant

c) Moment before the entrée arrives

d) Moment to take a break

2) The Customer Waiting List must include

a) all dining reservations for that day

b) the name of the party, the number of people in the party, the time stated to the party for the next open table, and the exact time of this statement to the party

c) parties of four or less

d) the list of waitstaff that customers often request

3) The Employee Position List is made up of

a) all the names of the waitstaff in the restaurant that day

b) all the names of the kitchen employees that day

c) all the dining room service staff names and their respective positions in the restaurant for that shift

d) all the names of the managers and hosts that day

4) The Employee Position List should be listed on the Daily Reservation Sheet and posted

    a) every day

    b) before each and every shift

    c) beginning each month

    d) once a week

5) The Host can help gauge the evenness of customer traffic flow to each waitperson in the dining room by

    a) recording the number of guests seated per waitstation on paper

    b) looking for the waitstation that is busiest

    c) seeing how busy the bussers are

    d) putting reservation cards on all of the front tables

6) The best way the Host can balance the dining room seating is to

    a) seat customers in the back of the restaurant first

    b) "stagger" customer seating by allotting an even number of diners (approximately) to each waitperson and recording it on the Daily Reservation Sheet

    c) seat early customers near the bar

    d) seat early customers in the front of the restaurant to the fastest waitperson

7) The best way to answer the telephone in a restaurant would be

    a) Hello!

    b) Thank you for calling the "Blue Café," may I help you?

    c) Good Evening!

    d) all three answers.

8) When taking a reservation, one must ask for

a) the name of the party and arrival time

b) the name of the party, number of people in the party, and arrival time

c) the name of the party, date, number of people in the party, and arrival time

d) the name of the party, date, number of people in the party, arrival time, and contact phone number.

9) If a party is late for their reservation and has not called the restaurant, their table should be held for

a) 15 minutes

b) ½ an hour

c) 1 hour

d) whatever the Host's discretion is depending on factors such as time of day, number of people currently on the waiting list, etc.

10) In an extremely busy restaurant, the best way to keep newly arriving customers from leaving to dine elsewhere is to:

a) offer menus to waiting customers to pass the time

b) tell the customers that the wait time for an open table is less than what it really is

c) appear hurried at the Front Door of the restaurant

d) politely ask customers to step over to the bar or waiting area, offer menus to pass the time, and possibly offer some complimentary items (bar snacks, simple appetizers, cocktails, etc.) to keep them from leaving the restaurant

11) Define No-Show:

   a) a staff member who does not show up for work

   b) a party does not inform the restaurant that they are canceling a reservation

   c) a customer does not show up for a party

   d) No beverage delivery that day

12) Large parties (approximately ten people or more) should

   a) be asked politely to reconfirm their reservation

   b) in smaller restaurants, be asked to leave a deposit

   c) always be treated with special attention

   d) all three answers

13) With regards to outdoor dining, reservations should not be taken because

   a) when the weather is nice for outdoor dining, no-shows will hurt business

   b) holding empty outdoor tables for reservations while eager customers are waiting to dine outdoors will hurt business

   c) if the customer especially needs to make a reservation, most likely it can be made for the indoor dining area

   d) all three answers.

14) At the Front Door, the Host's main objective is to

   a) seat customers as fast as humanly possible

   b) use creative ways to maximize table usage while minimizing costly service mistakes in the dining room

   c) always look completely relaxed and unfazed

   d) not have a cigarette

15) Menu knowledge is very important to the waitstaff for providing excellent service because

a) customers can be alerted to dietary restrictions

b) it is essential for the up selling of menu items.

c) customers have more confidence in a knowledgeable and helpful waitperson

d) all three answers

16) For maximum usage and efficiency, the menu descriptions must

a) be posted in an inconspicuous area to be used for quick reference by the waitstaff

b) include all of the major ingredients in the dishes on the menu

c) be printed up clearly and made available to all waitstaff and food-runners with extra copies made available for new employees

d) all three answers

17) Customer position points are

a) the exact placement of each seated diner with respect to the table number

b) the exact time a customer arrives

c) mainly in the front area where customers are seated

d) customers who are facing the back of the restaurant

18) For maximum usage and efficiency, the dining room floor diagrams including table numbers and position points must be

a) printed up clearly, posted in an area for quick reference, and handed out to all dining room staff with extra copies available for all new employees

b) kept only as a final reference for any disputes

c) posted in the restaurant office area to be used for quick access

d) answers b and c only

19) The dining room tables should be numbered by beginning each column or row with the number

a) 11, 21, 31, 41

b) 14, 24, 34, 44

c) 15, 25, 35, 45

d) 1, 10, 20, 30

20) The dining room service schedule must be

a) printed up clearly and made available for all dining room staff

b) posted in an area for easy viewing by the staff

c) made available and posted by Thursday/Friday for the following week beginning on Sunday

d) all three answers

21) The dining room service schedule should be done by

a) anyone willing to put the time in

b) the owner or top manager in charge

c) either owner/manager or experienced waitperson that has great communicative abilities with the staff

d) the chef

22) When making up the staff schedule one must

a) forecast, as best as possible, the incoming business into the restaurant for each shift of the week

b) take all seasonal aspects of the business and location into consideration

c) stay in close communication with the dining room service staff at all times

d) all three answers

23) The best way to balance the staff schedule is to

a) hire a lot of people and under staff

b) have each employee work a balance of at least three to four shifts per week

c) keep a small staff and let everyone work overtime

d) all three answers

24) An example of how the schedule directly affects payroll and the dining room service would be if

a) too many staff members are scheduled on a slow day of business

b) too few staff members are scheduled on a busy day

c) the schedule is done poorly every week resulting in low staff morale (which eventually gets transferred to the customer)

d) all three answers

25) The best way for the staff to communicate their schedule requests to the schedule maker is to

a) tell the schedule maker verbally

b) tell another manager who does not make the schedule

c) write down the schedule requests on a posted sheet of paper or hand a small sheet of paper with requests to the schedule maker

d) cross off other names on the schedule and put your name

26) The purpose of the Staff Substitution Book is for

a) meal substitutions for the staff

b) customer service relations

c) dining room service staff substitutions which are signed by the staff members involved and, then, initialed by a manager

d) management shift changes

27) Sidework is

a) the opening preparations and closing down of dining room service

b) the work done by personnel outside of the restaurant

c) the duty list, which should be printed up clearly for each position and posted for easy viewing by all staff.

d) a and c only

28) If an employee's sidework is to bring up light food items from downstairs, then this employee should *not* be

a) watching the front door to seat early arriving customers

b) the only employee answering the phone for reservations

c) going across the street to the store

d) all three answers

29) Cross-training helps form a well rounded staff because

a) employees will empathize with each other's work positions

b) it keeps the job more interesting and increases labor productivity

c) it gives employees more confidence as they take on added work responsibilities

d) all three answers.

30) Cross-training should be for approximately what percentage of the staff?

a) 80%

b) 50%

c) 15%

d) 100%

31) Define the Huddle-up:

a) A general staff meeting once per month

b) A management meeting once per week

c) A dining room service staff meeting only

d) A meeting, before each shift, between the dining room service staff and management to discuss restaurant-related issues, change, and updates

32) Dining room temperature, lighting, and music should be adjusted

a) slowly (with customers barely noticing) while paying attention to the needs of the dining room, time of day, and theme of the restaurant

b) according to the manager's mood

c) always warm, loud, and bright

d) to always save money

33) An example of dining room staff and management working together as a team is

a) a waitperson with no tables refusing to seat a newly arrived customer

b) a host taking a drink order, but forgetting to tell the waitperson

c) a waitperson taking a reservation for next Sunday Brunch over the telephone and recording it properly in the Reservation Journal

d) a waitperson (not busy) refusing to give assistance to a fellow waitperson in desperate need of help because of station overloading

34) Waitstaff can be rewarded by management if they

a) have consistently high check averages

b) consistently give exceptional customer service

c) are always helping out the host and management

d) all three answers.

35) Customer needs can be coordinated and communicated to the staff quickly by

a) pointing fingers to identify customer needs

b) clearly speaking through the table numbers and position points

c) describing the person's dress or facial features

d) all three answers

36) The person who has the most right of way when passing by is

a) the person carrying three hot pasta plates

b) the person carrying two drinks

c) the tallest person

d) the person carrying a bread basket

37) A restaurant phrase to warn people nearby of one's presence would be

a) "behind you"

b) "watch your back"

c) "passing through"

d) all three answers

38) If a waitperson is on a slow line for service (computer use, bar, coffee, etc.), then the waitperson should

a) talk to other employees

b) watch other employees

c) leave the long line and move to a shorter line, or try to perform another task in the meantime until the long line dwindles

d) watch the TV

39) Sanitation is very important in foodservice because

    a) it directly affects the health of the diners

    b) it directly affects the health of the employees

    c) customers will not enter a restaurant with poor sanitary conditions

    d) all three answers

40) All staff members must

    a) be washing hands frequently throughout shift (always after using the restroom or smoking)

    b) wear a clean and pressed uniform

    c) be well groomed with clean fingernails and long hair pulled back

    d) all three answers

41) When carrying a glass, fingers must never touch

    a) the stem

    b) the inside of the glass and/or the outside upper lip of the glass—anywhere the diner's mouth can touch

    c) the base

    d) all three answers

42) When carrying a plate, fingers must never touch

    a) the bottom

    b) the sides

    c) the inside of the plate—anywhere the food can come in contact

    d) the underside

43) When scooping out ice, it's best to use

    a) a metal/plastic scoop or pitcher

    b) a glass

    c) the hands

    d) a napkin

44) A great way to cut down on glass and plate ware breakage is to

    a) put the glass/plate wares in the bus pans slowly

    b) use two separately labeled buspans, one for glass ware and one for plate ware

    c) put the glass wares off to the side of the plate wares

    d) answers a and b only

45) All areas in the restaurant should be clean and free of clutter, especially near the Front Door because

    a) it may prevent customers from entering the restaurant

    b) it is unsafe

    c) bits of food on the floor or rug can attract pests

    d) all three answers

46) If a glass breaks on the floor, it should be

    a) picked up with the hands

    b) (if very large pieces) picked up with thick gloves or napkins while other small pieces can be swept up with a broom and dustpan

    c) kicked to the side

    d) answers b and c only

47) If a very heavy object must be moved, one should

a) do it alone

b) ask for help get the task done

c) use a dolly cart or two wheeled cart to transport the object

d) b and c only

48) The best way to understand and handle safety issues is to

a) anticipate any potential hazards while trying to prevent or figure out how to deal with any unsafe situations (ahead of time if possible)

b) deal with the problems only after the fact

c) try not to pay attention until it happens

d) start writing down facts while the incident is still occurring

49) If there is an emergency incident in the restaurant, the interviewing process should not begin until

a) one hour has passed

b) the emergency personnel has left the scene

c) the emergency situation has calmed down and medical treatment has been dispensed

d) immediately after the incident

50) The emergency and safety items needed to be in stock at all times are

a) emergency telephone numbers (police, fire depts., ambulance, hospital, and other major numbers for the area) posted for easy viewing

b) working fire extinguishers, CPR kits

c) First aid medical kit: band-aids, gauze pads, adhesive tape, antibacterial spray, and burn spray

d) all three answers

ANSWERS with EXPLANATIONS

1) a

   Moments of Truth, always happening in the business world, are the opportunities to make a lasting, positive impression on the customer which is extremely important to service reputation.

2) b

   The Waiting list helps the Host keep track of time and parties eagerly awaiting an open table.

3) c

   The Employee Position List informs everyone working in the dining room about their respective employee positions for each and every shift.

4) b

   The Employee Position List provides much needed dining room information for proper communication especially during the busy hours.

5) a

   The dining room should be sat as evenly as possible without overloading any one section or waitperson at a time. If the Host records the seating allotment for each waitstation, it will help balance the seating process tremendously.

6) b

   The dining room should be sat as evenly as possible without overloading any one section or waitperson at a time. If the Host records the seating allotment for each waitstation, it will help balance the seating process tremendously.

7) b

Proper phone answering is an immediate reflection on the restaurant's customer service as first impressions are lasting impressions.

8) d

Whenever taking a reservation, one must get all of the pertinent information from the customer.

9) d

It is always best to use proper judgment and common sense when making decisions in the dining room.

10) d

When working the Front Door, the Host must go the distance to save any customers from leaving to dine elsewhere. Once customers are lost, they could be lost forever.

11) b

No-Shows will hurt business especially during busy times.

12) d

For large party reservations, always try to get reconfirmation as extreme care must be taken for the party's sake and the restaurant's sake.

13) d

Outdoor dining almost always works better on a "first come, first serve" basis

14) b

When working the Front Door, one must use creative ways to maximize table usage and minimize costly dining room service mistakes.

15) d

The menu is a waitperson's sales product. For any salesperson, one of the most important assets is to know the product—inside and out.

16) d

The waitstaff always needs to have quick access to the menu descriptions to help sell and up sell the product, especially new hires.

17) a

Using Customer Position Points will enhance dining room service facilitating food and beverage delivery as well.

18) a

Dining room floor diagrams facilitate the communication and delivery of dining service by exacting all waitstations, table numbers, and position points. The floor diagrams should be posted properly and made available to all staff.

19) a

The initial numbers starting with the number 1 are easiest to speak, hear and work with.

20) d

The schedule is a major part of the restaurant and the employee's work and lives, so great care must be taken when creating it.

21) c

Whoever makes up the schedule should have excellent knowledge of the dining room operations and close communication with the staff.

22) d

The dining room staff schedule is tied directly to dining room service, and influenced by many different factors

23) b

In making up the dining room service staff schedule, for each and every shift, there must be a balance of labor matching the needs of the forecasted business for the dining room. Over the course of time, improper scheduling lowers staff morale, which eventually gets transferred to the customers.

24) d

In making up the dining room service staff schedule, for each and every shift, there must be a balance of labor matching the needs of the forecasted business for the dining room. Over the course of time, improper scheduling can lower staff morale, which eventually gets transferred to the customers.

25) c

The dining room service schedule is a complicated task, so the staff should communicate schedule requests clearly and concisely to the schedule maker.

26) c

The substitution book, overseen by the management, ensures that all employee shifts will be properly covered for the restaurant week in and week out.

27) d

Sidework ensures the staff with all of the necessary tools to give proper dining room service, and should be posted for all staff to easily view.

28) d

The Sidework duties should coincide with each waitstation location, if possible.

29) d

Cross-training broadens restaurant talents and increases staff versatility to help ensure excellent dining room service.

30) c

For Cross-Training, 15% (give or take a few points) works best. A percentage too low will not have a great effect and too high may become costly.

31) d

The Huddle-up helps the workshift run smoother because of better communication amongst employees and management.

32) a

Air temperature, lighting and music must always be adjusted with care to create the best atmosphere for diners.

33) c

Dining room tasks always overlap, therefore; an atmosphere of everyone helping each other must be created to produce a "positive domino effect throughout the restaurant."

34) d

Staff members who are rewarded for their excellence will inspire other employees to give great customer service as well.

35) b

Teaching the staff to communicate through the table numbers and position points adds to the organization and efficiency of the dining room service and looks good too.

36) a

The person carrying the heaviest weight or most dangerous items (hot coffee, pasta etc.) always gets the right of passage. It is safe and courteous.

37) d

Since restaurants usually have tight spaces, it is best to politely speak up and inform when necessary using the proper "phrases."

38) c

Waitstaff and all employees should always seek to multi-task to save time, motion, and energy while performing service.

39) d

Keeping a restaurant clean and safe is a very important part of dining room customer service along with the obvious health reasons.

40) d

Personal hygiene is very important for health reasons. It is a reflection of dining room customer service and the restaurant itself.

41) b

Holding glass ware correctly is sanitary and proper dining service.

42) c

Holding plate ware correctly is sanitary and proper dining service.

43) a

Sanitation and safety are very important concepts in dining room service, restaurants, and life.

44) d

Cutting down on breakage is not only an important safety precaution, but it saves the restaurant on inventory costs. Dining wares should always be handled carefully and kept separated whenever possible.

45) d

Sanitation and Safety are a very important part of dining room service, restaurants, and life.

46) b

Sanitation and Safety are a very important part of dining room service, restaurants, and life.

47) d

Using good judgment and care measures for Safety is a very important part of restaurants.

48) a

Using good judgment and care measures for Safety is a very important part of restaurants.

49) c

Using good judgment and care measures for Safety is a very important part of restaurants.

50) d

Using good judgment and care measures for Safety is a very important part of restaurants.

Topserve Consulting

Restaurant Performance Evaluation Guide ©

Please rate each category using the following point system by answering in the corresponding box. Comment on each point using the back pages if necessary.

1 – Poor   2 – Fair   3 – Good   4 – Very Good   5 – Excellent

A. Restaurant Appearance (outside): Overall location and look:	
1) Did the restaurant have nice imagery and positioning at first glance? (walk-by view /drive-by view?)	
2) Was the outdoor signage appropriate, visible, and well-lit?	
3) How was the outdoor lighting?	
4) Were the windows clean?	
5) Were the sidewalks swept clean and the trash removed?	
6) Was the front entrance clear and uncluttered?	

7) Was the menu visible with a nice look?	
8) Was there a creative use of plants?	
9) Was there easy access parking or a valet service?	
10) Was there wheelchair accessibility?	
Comments:	

B. Restaurant Appearance (inside): Front door, Reservation desk and host/maître d' performance:	
1) Were the front door/desk, coat check, and patron waiting areas clean, clear, and uncluttered?	
2) How was the initial telephone inquiry and reservation handled by the host and/or staff? (prompt, helpful and courteous?)	
3) Did the host have a neat, clean, and upbeat appearance?	
4) What was the initial greeting, reservation taking and seating like? (prompt, helpful, energetic, and courteous?)	
Comments:	

C. Ambiance:	
1) Describe the dining room décor, lighting, music, etc. (overall atmosphere and theme).	
2) Was it a comfortable atmosphere conducive to relaxation and enjoyable dining?	
3) Were customer and employee traffic flows uncluttered and easily mobile?	
Comments:	

D. Dining Room Appearance:	
1) Was the carpet/floor clean and uncluttered?	
2) Were the tables and chairs clean and sturdy with a nice look?	
3) Did the tables, chairs, and linens match and have an orderly arrangement?	
4) Were the linens/table tops, silverware settings, glassware, and plate ware clean?	
5) Did the above match and have an orderly arrangement?	
6) Describe the ceiling, fixtures, drapes, plants, and pictures/paintings (crooked or straight)?	
7) Was the indoor signage (especially the bathroom and exit signs) appropriate, visible, and well-lit?	
Comments:	
E. Waitperson Appearance/Presence/Approach:	
1) How was the overall waitperson appearance? (neat with a clean uniform?)	
2) How was the initial approach to the table and customer greeting? (prompt and courteous?)	
3) Drink order taking: Was the waitperson knowledgeable and helpful with the beverages and wine menu?	
4) Was there highlighting and up selling of the beverages and of wine?	
5) Food order taking: Was the waitperson knowledgeable and helpful with the menu and food?	
6) Was there highlighting and up selling of the menu?	
7) Was there an announcement of the daily specials?	
8) Was there help with food and wine pairing?	

9) How was the waitperson's overall energy, organization, efficiency, timing, speed, communication, and speech?	
Comments:	

F. Menu Evaluation; Food and beverage quality:	
1) Were the menus clean with a nice appearance?	
2) Was the menu consistent with the dining room theme, décor, color, and overall atmosphere?	
3) Was the menu balanced and easy to read with proper product placement and pricing?	
4) Were there descriptive adjectives used on the menu to describe dishes?	
5) Were there any signature menu items?	
6) Were there separate menus for appetizers/entrees, dessert, and wine?	
7) Was there a special bar, beverage, or martini menu?	
8) Describe the overall beverage presentation, freshness, taste, pour volume, and garnishes. (quality and quantity?)	
9) Describe the overall food presentation, freshness, taste, texture, temperature, and portion size. (quality and quantity?)	
Comments:	

G. Food and Beverage Service including Table Maintenance:	
1) Was there a proper and timely offering of beverage/water refill?	
2) Was the plate/silverware distributed properly for food service? (large spoon for soup, small fork for shellfish, etc.?)	

3) Was there a proper and timely offering of condiments? (fresh pepper, grated cheese, ketchup, mustard, etc.)	
4) How was the plate/glassware handling and clearing technique? (smooth and sanitary?)	
5) Were the silverware and linens replaced when necessary?	
6) Was the table crumbed after the courses/ meal? (when applicable)	
7) How was the waitperson's overall food and beverage serving technique? (smooth and sanitary?)	
8) Was there an anticipation of the customer's needs throughout the meal?	
Comments:	
H. Dessert, After Dinner Drink, Coffee/Tea Suggestion and Service:	
1) Was there proper timing after the meal by the waitperson to begin offering coffee and dessert service?	
2) Was the table properly cleared before coffee and dessert service?	
3) Was the plate/silverware distributed properly and timely for coffee and dessert service?	
Apply the above performance evaluation points (#E, F, and G) to coffee and dessert service.	
Comments:	
I. Ending the Meal and Handling the Method of Payment:	
1) Was there a proper pricing, calculation and appearance of the check? Was the check placed inside a nice looking booklet??	
2) Was the check returned in a timely manner?	

3) Did the waitperson or any dining staff mention any special events or promotions featured by the restaurant?	
4) How was the restaurant exit? Did anybody thank you and say goodbye?	

Comments:

J. Dining Room Service Staff / Management Interaction and Conduct Towards the Customers and Each Other:

1) Was there a good rapport between the dining room staff and customers?	
2) Did the staff communicate and work well with each other on the dining room floor?	
3) Were the staff helping each other with overlapping dining room tasks and customer needs, regardless of positions held (manager, host, waitperson, runner, busser, etc.)?	
4) Was there balance and consistency in connecting each entity of the restaurant departments (bar, kitchen, dining room) and staff (manager, host, wait staff, runner, busser, etc.)?	

Comments:

K. Restroom Facility Upkeep:

1) Was there proper signage leading towards the restrooms?	
2) In the restrooms, were the surfaces, mirrors, walls and floors clean?	
3) Had the overstuffed trash been removed?	
4) Was there a good soap, air freshener and paper supply?	

The restrooms must be well ventilated and CLEAN, CLEAN, CLEAN.

Comments:

Comments:

_____

_____

_____

_____

_____

_____

_____

_____

_____

_____

_____

_____

_____

About the Author

Richard Saporito has over 30 years of restaurant service experience in many large, diverse, and profitable New York City establishments. He uses this successful experience to help restaurants achieve their desired customer service goals—understanding that it may be the difference between success and failure. Read more about his company's products and services, both dedicated to restaurant development and improvement, by visiting the website below.

www.topserveconsulting.com

Lightning Source UK Ltd.
Milton Keynes UK
18 March 2011

169480UK00002B/122/P